Scat Singing Method

Beginning
Vocal Improvisation

by

Dr. Scott Fredrickson

ScottMusicPublications
www.scottmusic.com

Scott Music Publications
www.scottmusic.com

Printed in the United States of America

Library of Congress Cataloging-in-Publication Data

ISBN 0-9620177-0-1

Scott*MusicPublications*
www.scottmusic.com

Acknowledgements

Many thanks to the following people who assisted in the production of this project. Without their help, this method would not have happened.

Doug Anderson	Audrey Grier	Dan Radlauer
Bill Anchutz	Gene Grier	Dan Schwartz
Norm Boaz	Michael Harvey	Dave Siebels
Wayne Cook	Dr. John Kuzmich	Dr. Andrew Smith
Sandra Cryder	Larry Lapin	Doug Strawn
Frank DeMiero	Roger Letson	Carl Strommen
Roger Emerson	Gary Martin	Peter Taylor
Dr. Sandy Feldstein	Gary McRoberts	Rich Watson
Dr. Darwin Fredrickson	Dr. Milt Olsson	Dave Wells
Norine Fredrickson	John O'Reilly	Sue Woodhams

I would especially like to thank my wonderful wife Elizabeth for helping me edit this new edition.

The Vocal Jazz movement is growing by leaps and bounds. Hundreds of new groups are being formed, and more choral directors are experimenting with Jazz in their programs. As I traveled throughout the United States and Canada adjudicating festivals and working with groups in clinic situations, I became aware of a lack of understanding of the techniques of vocal improvisation. The Scat Singing Method was written in hopes of solving this problem. The techniques presented in this book have been tested on hundreds of choral directors and thousands of students across the United States and Canada. I hope the ideas and concepts work as well for you as they did for them.

The Scat Singing Method has been designed to teach you the basic techniques of vocal improvisation. It allows for instant success by providing a model for Scat technique (recorded and transcribed), and then provides the opportunity to practice that technique with the same recorded rhythm section that is recorded on the enclosed CD. Included are eight tunes which can be used to practice the techniques you have learned.

Do not rush through the method. Stop and repeat sections over and over if you need to. Take your time. If you plan to use the method in your classroom, go through the entire method first, before you present it to your students. By attaining an overall understanding of the method, you will be able to do a better job of teaching scat singing.

I wish you the best in your new musical endeavor, and most of all, keep scattin'.

Table of Contents

I. Contents

Each Scat Singing Method includes complete instructions with examples, eight performable compositions and arrangements which include melody with SAB back-up parts, written-out piano, bass and drum parts, and two CDs which contain:

CD 1:

Complete instructions with examples of all concepts discussed. Each musical example is performed twice for your listening. Immediately following each example, is an opportunity to practice that concept with the recorded rhythm section. It is recommended that you listen to the entire CD before trying the techniques taught in the method. By doing this, you will have a better understanding of the total concept of the method.

CD 2:

Eight new performable compositions and arrangements in various styles, tempos and keys. Each piece has rhythm section, vocal melody, SAB back-up parts and no recorded scat solo. These are the pieces with which you practice and possibly perform the concepts you will learn in this method.

Each tune is repeated six times.
  1 & 2 Melody and rhythm section.
  3 & 4 Vocal back-up parts and rhythm section.
  5 & 6 Melody and vocal back-up parts and rhythm section.

1. *Scat Blues*	Fast blues	Medium	CD 2 - Track 14
2. *Railroad Rock*	Rock	Easy	CD 2 - Track 15
3. *Shuffle the Deck*	Jazz shuffle	Easy	CD 2 - Track 16
4. *When the Saints Get Down*	Swing	Easy	CD 2 - Track 17
5. *Swingin' at the Riverside*	Swing	Easy	CD 2 - Track 18
6. *New Bossa*	Bossa nova	Medium	CD 2 - Track 19
7. *Take the Alternate "A" Train*	Fast swing	Difficult	CD 2 - Track 20
8. *Syncopated Samba*	Samba	Difficult	CD 2 - Track 21

Separate recorded rhythm tracks for each practice tune are available separately. Please contact Scott Music Publications for more information.

CD 1 - Track 1

II. Introduction

Scat singing or vocal improvisation can be one of the most satisfying forms of creativity for singers. **You** can learn to do it and teach it, even if you have never done it before. The key to scat singing is **intelligent listening**. All you have to do is use your ears, your intelligence, and your voice.

This Scat Singing Method uses an aural/melodic approach rather than a theoretical approach to improvisation. This means that you will be **listening** to the words, rhythms, harmonies and phrases etc., **imitating** the examples, and **experimenting** with the recorded rhythm section and singers. After you have gained proficiency at scat singing, you should be able more readily to understand the theoretical relationships that exist between the melodic and harmonic materials.

As you move from using syllables, to melody, to rhythm, etc. in this method, make sure that you follow the directions and steps in order. You must master each isolated musical element before moving on to the next. Later in the method you should be able to integrate these concepts, and be able to use a little of each of them at the same time.

All of the examples, included with this method, will use the tune *Scat Blues*. This tune is included in the list of practice tunes. The *Scat Blues* is a 12-bar Blues melody that can be quickly learned and easily used to practice the concepts contained in the method. When you have completed all of the sections using the *Scat Blues* as your model, you may go back through the entire method using either one of the practice tunes or a tune of your own choosing.

III. Syllables

**The first step in learning to scat sing is creating
new syllables over a melody.**

A. Sing the original melody of the tune *Scat Blues* using the syllables *du* and
dut. Notice that the syllable *du* is used on the longer note values, and
the syllable *dut* is used on the shorter note values.

Example 1

CD 1 - Track 3

In all of the following exercises when you are asked to sing using the syllable *du*, use either *du* or *dut* depending on the length of the note.

B. Sing the melody alternating the syllables *du vee* (pronounced *doo vee*). Some of the short note values in this example are now long. This is the result of the long syllables *du* and *vee* being sung on previously short note values.

Example 2

CD 1 - Track 4

Did you notice that when you alternated *du* and *vee* exactly as notated, some of the stylistic articulations and inflections just didn't "feel right"?

C. Sing the syllables *shu bee du bee* alternating between *straight* eighth notes, and *swing style* eighth notes.

Example 3

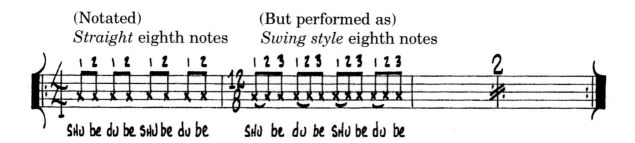

The use of *du vee* and other similar syllable pairs (*du bah*, *shu bee du bee*) is usually used in Vocal Jazz *swing style* to highlight the fact that the second of two eighth notes (the last 1/3 of the beat) should be louder than the first (the first 2/3 of the beat). The use of the softer *du* on the longer note and the brighter *vee* on the shorter note naturally makes the second note "pop out". This is one of the major stylistic elements that makes *swing style* jazz so unique.

CD 1 - Track 5

D. Sing the melody using the syllables *du vee*, but this time don't just alternate them, sing them where YOU think they "feel better."

Notice how the following example *feels better* when the *du's* and the *vee's* are sung in a more *appropriate* place for *swing style*.

Example 4

CD 1 - Track 6

E. Sing the melody and make up a few of your own syllables along with *du* and *du vee*.

Remember, singing *du* and *du vee* along with **a few** other syllables on the melody, can make for a very satisfying and appealing scat solo. Simplicity is usually the best choice.

Here are a few syllable suggestions that are long sounds: *vu, du, shu, wee, vee, zee, bee, vah, bah, dah, dwee* and *skwee*.

Here are a few syllable suggestions that are short sounds: *bop, dop, vop, dot, bot, zot,* and *dit.*

It is common choral diction to sing *bah-puh* for the syllable *bop*, and *di-tuh* for the syllable *dit*. The usual jazz interpretation is to sing these types of short sounds as **one syllable sounds,** by stopping the air either with the tongue or the lips.

Use the appropriate length of syllable sound when singing long or short note values. For example, sing *du* on a whole note, and *dot* on an eighth note if followed by an eighth rest.

Practice these syllables, and others, until you find the ones that *feel right* for a particular rhythmic articulation or inflection that you desire.

CD 1 - Track 7

Example 5

CD 1 - Track 8

F. Sing the melody and gradually make up all of you own syllables.

(It is important at this step to discipline yourself when altering only the syllables, and make sure that you do not change the original melody and rhythms.)

Example 6

**PROFICIENCY SHOULD BE ATTAINED ON EACH STEP
BEFORE MOVING ONTO THE NEXT STEP**

CD 1 - Track 9

IV. Melody

The second step in learning to scat sing is altering and embellishing the melody. This means adding and substituting notes, sounds, or effects to the original notes to the melody.

A. Sing the original melody of the tune using the syllable *du*.

This brings you back to *ground zero*, so that when the new concept is presented, you can easily relate it to the original melody.

Example 7

CD 1 - Track 10

B. Sing the original melody using *du*, and add a new accent, inflection, or articulation in various places.

Tenuto:
Hold nearly full value with space before next note, unaccented.

Vertical Accent:
Strong accent, hold less than full value.

Staccato:
Short, detached, unaccented.

Example 8

CD 1 - Track 11

C. Sing the melody on *du*, and add a *fall-off* or *ascending smear*.

Fall-off:
A rapid descending
slide starting on
the note. (Usually
followed by a rest.)

Ascending Smear:
A rapid ascending
slide starting before
and below the note.

Example 9

D. Sing the melody on *du*, and add **a few** more embellishments such as varying dynamics, an *ascending glissando*, *plop*, *doit*, *ghost note*, *shake*, or *flip*.

Ascending Glissando:
Upward slide between two pitches.

Plop:
A rapid descending slide starting before and above the note.

Example 10

CD 1 - Track 13

Doit:
A rapid ascending smear
after the note is sounded.

Ghost Note:
Indefinite pitch, more of a
rhythmic pulse than a note.

Example 11

CD 1 - Track 14

Shake:
A variation of the tone, upwards much like an exaggerated trill.

Flip:
Sing the note, raise the pitch and drop into the following note.

Example 12

CD 1 - Track 15

E. Now, while singing *du*, change several notes of the melody.

Make sure that you maintain the original rhythm.

Example 13

F. While singing *du*, **gradually** change more of the original melody. Make sure that you do not change the original rhythms.

(One of the keys to success with this method is to maintain the self discipline to alter only one element at a time.)

Example 14

CD 1 - Track 17

G. While singing *du*, change **more** of the original melody and add more of your own embellishments.

Example 15

H. As you change more and more of the notes of the melody and add more embellishments, **always keep the original melody in mind**. If all else fails, you still know where you are in the melody and can sing it using the syllable *du*.

CD 1 - Track 18

V. Rhythm

The third step in learning to scat sing is altering and embellishing the rhythms of the original melody.

A. Sing the original melody on *du*.

This will bring you back to *ground zero* again.

Example 16

CD 1 - Track 19

B. Sing the melody on *du*, and create **a few** of your own rhythms.

Always make sure that you do not change the melody.

Keep your rhythmic changes simple.

Example 17

CD 1 - Track 20

C. Sing the melody on *du*, and **gradually** change more of the rhythms and add some off-beat accents.

Make sure that you maintain the original melody.

Example 18

CD 1 - Track 21

D. Sing the melody on *du*, and make up all of your own rhythms.

Always keep the original melody.

Example 19

CD 1 - Track 22

VI. Integration

The integration of the preceding musical elements is the most fun and the most important section of this method.

There is a natural tendency at this point to be overly confident with the use of the three previously isolated concepts (Syllables, Melody, and Rhythm). If you have not **MASTERED** each concept, **DO NOT PROCEED**. Go back and review the material until each concept is fully understood and **MASTERED**. You must discipline yourself during this section, and integrate the elements as directed; otherwise, you will not achieve the desired proficiency, or the understanding of the logic and development of a good scat solo.

When doing the following examples, do EXACTLY what you are asked to do. Do not do any more, or any less.

CD 1 - Track 23

A. Melody and Rhythm
(syllable *du* is constant)

1. Start singing the melody on *du*, and change a few notes of the melody, and one or two rhythms.

Do not add any new syllables at this point.

Example 20

CD 1 - Track 24

2. Proceed gradually by adding more of your own melody notes, embellishments and rhythms.

Sing only *du* during this section.

Example 21

CD 1 - Track 25

B. Syllables and Melody
(rhythm is constant)

1. Start singing the melody on *du*, and change a few of the melody notes and add a few embellishments and a couple of new syllables.

Do not change the original rhythms.

Example 22

CD 1 - Track 26

2. Proceed gradually by adding more of your own notes and embellishments and creating new syllables.

Maintain the original rhythms.

Example 23

CD 1 - Track 27

C. Syllables and Rhythm
(melody is constant)

1. Start singing the melody on *du*, and change one or two of the rhythms and add a few new syllables.

Do not change the original melody.

Example 24

CD 1 - Track 28

2. Proceed gradually by adding more of your own rhythms and syllables.

Maintain the original melody.

Example 25

CD 1 - Track 29

D. Syllables, Melody, and Rhythm

1. Proceed as you have been, but this time include all three elements as you start singing on *du*.

Keep it simple at first.

Example 26

CD 1 - Track 30

2. **Gradually** increase the amount of your own material in the solo.

Example 27

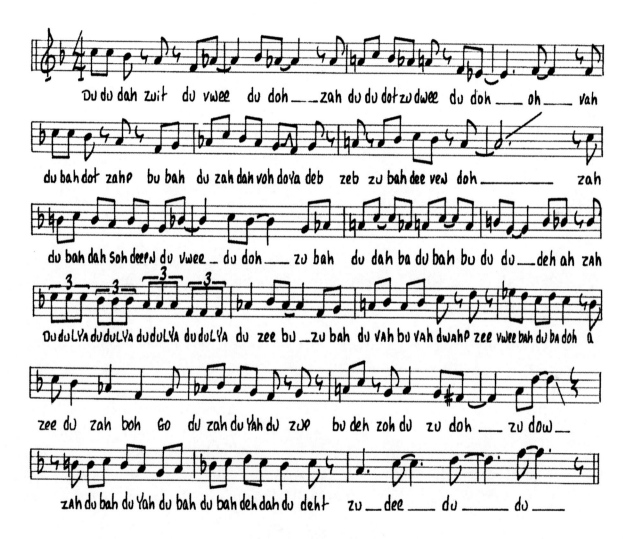

Remember, if you do not isolate the elements and practice them separately, you will not achieve the proficiency that you desire in vocal improvisation.

CD 1 - Track 31

VII. Phrases

If the phrases are constructed properly, even the simplest scat solo can be exciting.

Musical forms are constructed of phrases. Usually the basic idea or motif is presented in the first phrase. The second phrase grows logically out of the first, the third grows out of the first and second, the fourth grows out of the first, second and third, etc., with each phrase contributing to the overall development of the musical form. The number of phrases in a musical form can vary from three 4-bar phrases in a 12-bar Blues, to four 8-bar phrases in many popular tunes, to dozens of phrases in some larger works.

This is one way to build a good phrase.

A. Start your solo softly in the lower register with common syllables (such as *du* etc.), with few notes, or with notes of longer value, and with simple rhythms.

B. Gradually increase the dynamics, the uniqueness of your syllables, the intensity of the rhythms, always aiming at the peak of the phrase.

C. About three quarters of the way (or more) through your solo, reach the highest and most complex section of the music. Gradually taper off the volume and range, simplify your syllables, increase note values, and lessen the intensity of the rhythms. This will tend to release the tension that you have created, and bring you back to your starting point.

12-Bar Blues Form

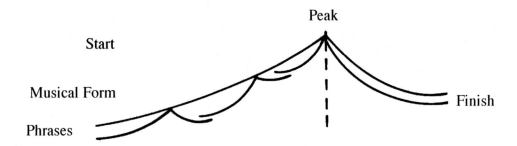

CD 2 - Track 1

Example 28

Occasionally, a phrase will build and peak into the *shout chorus* section of a tune. Build as before, but move the peak of the phrase closer to the end. This will tend to *set up* the next phrase (The *shout chorus* section) at a much higher level of complexity and excitement.

CD 2 - Track 2

D. Now, refer back to the 12-bar Blues form chart (on page 36), and notice the relationship of the phrases as they build within themselves, and together build to the overall peak of the larger musical form.

The following example builds to a peak using only dynamics as the changing element.

Example 29

CD 2 - Track 3

VIII. Rehearsal Techniques & Ideas

A. Aural Imagery

Aural Imagery can lead to new sounds and syllables in scat singing. Try producing sounds of abstract ideas and unrelated things. This will cause you to explore new areas of imaginative sounds.

1. Scat sing using only wooden sounds, glass sounds, trumpet sounds, red sounds, blue sounds, saxophone sounds, etc., or any other unrelated or abstract sounds.

Example 30

CD 2 - Track 4

2. Explore the various sounds produced within the mouth using only the front of the tongue, back of the tongue, lips, teeth, tongue and lips, nasal cavities, changing shapes of the mouth cavity with the lips, etc. Be creative.

Try to think of these sounds during your scat solo.

Example 31

You try to transcribe this one!

CD 2 - Track 5

B. Imitation and Ear Training

1. Clap a 2-bar rhythm, and have it repeated back exactly.

Example 32

CD 2 - Track 6

2. Gradually, increase the length of bars and complexity of the rhythms.

Example 33

CD 2 - Track 7

3. Scat two bars on *du*, and have someone else repeat it back exactly.

Example 34

CD 2 - Track 8

4. Gradually, increase the number of bars and the amount of new syllables in the solo, and have this repeated exactly. (Sing one octave lower if necessary)

Example 35

CD 2 - Track 9

C. Question and Answer

This is another good form of ear training.

1. Scat two bars on *du*, and have someone else answer you with a different but complimentary scat, not a copy of your scat as before.

Example 36

CD 2 - Track 10

2. **Gradually**, expand your scat question from two to four to possibly eight bars, and have someone else answer you. Always remember to build a good phrase when doing this.

Example 37

3. Set up a drama situation, and have two people scat a conversation over several phrases. (Example: two people in a lover's spat).

CD 2 - Track 11

D. Phrases

1. Listen to any pop or jazz tune, and notice how the melody of the tune starts, builds to a peak, and comes back down to the starting point.

2. Sing the melody of a tune you know, and build an exciting phrase out of it using only the syllable *du*. Always be aware of where the peak of the tune will be.

3. Sing the tune as before, but change the placement of the peak to some other bar. Notice how musically different the tune sounds.

4. Divide the bars of the tune into 2-bar fragments, and assign each fragment to a different person. Have each person sing his or her fragment in order of assignment. In order to build a good phrase, they must use team work, and they must listen.

5. Divide the tune into any combination of fragments, and do the same thing.

6. **Gradually**, get away from *du* and the melody, and start building your own scat phrase using the techniques previously learned. Use several people, small fragments of the phrase, and team work.

E. Creativity

Devise exercises to determine:

1. Who can create the most interesting and unique sounds or syllables.

2. Who can alter a given melody the best using only *du*.

3. Who can alter the rhythm of a given tune the best while singing the exact melody.

4. Which team of singers can develop the best scat phrase over a set of chords to which they know the melody.

CD 2 - Track 12

IX. Conclusion

Scat singing is a basic element of vocal jazz, and encourages individual creativity. It can be one of the most exciting and satisfying forms of musical expression.

Here are a few things to remember:

A. Keep the melody in your mind at all times, and be aware of how it relates to the chords of the tune. This will aid you as you later learn the theory (chord structure, scales, etc.) of improvisation.

B. Keep your solo simple and near the melody.

C. Always strive for a sense of logic and development in each musical phrase and in the entire improvisational section.

D. Always observe good vocal production, even when trying to imitate instruments or other sounds.

E. As you learn each new concept, use the *Scat Blues*. You may wish to copy exactly the recorded and written examples until you understand the concepts. Repeat them until you do.

F. Now, pick one of the tunes on the CD and go back to the beginning of the method. Work through each step of the method until you have **MASTERED** all of the concepts using this new tune. Do the same thing with another of the practice tunes, or a tune of your own choosing

G. Listen to as many professional jazz singers as you can, and compare their solos with the technique you have learned in this method.

CD 2 - Track 13

The following annotated scat solo is based on the tune *It Don't Mean A Thing*, written and arranged by Scott Fredrickson, and published by Scott Music Publications, available in three voicings.

Example 38

H. Remember, make sure that you **MASTER** each isolated musical element before moving on to the next.

I. Good luck, and good scattin'

X. Practice Tunes

Eight new performable compositions and arrangements in various styles, tempos and keys are included on CD #2. Each piece has rhythm section, vocal melody, SAB back-up parts and no recorded scat solo. These are the pieces with which you practice and possibly perform the concepts you have learned in this method.

Each tune is repeated six times.

      1 & 2 Melody and rhythm section.

      3 & 4 Vocal back-up parts and rhythm section.

      5 & 6 Melody and vocal back-up parts and rhythm section.

1. *Scat Blues*	Fast blues	Medium	CD 2 - Track 14
2. *Railroad Rock*	Rock	Easy	CD 2 - Track 15
3. *Shuffle the Deck*	Jazz shuffle	Easy	CD 2 - Track 16
4. *When the Saints Get Down*	Swing	Easy	CD 2 - Track 17
5. *Swingin' at the Riverside*	Swing	Easy	CD 2 - Track 18
6. *New Bossa*	Bossa nova	Medium	CD 2 - Track 19
7. *Take the Alternate "A" Train*	Fast swing	Difficult	CD 2 - Track 20
8. *Syncopated Samba*	Samba	Difficult	CD 2 - Track 21

Optional choral parts are available for the eight practice tunes. Each part contains all eight tunes (melody and SAB back-up parts). In addition, separate rhythm sections are also available. Each set contains all eight tunes. Please contact the Scott Music Publications for more information.

For those who wish to use this method in a classroom setting, the recorded rhythm section for each of the eight practice tunes is available separately. Please contact the Scott Music Publications for more information.

1. Scat Blues

2. Railroad Rock

CD 2 - Track 15

3. Shuffle The Deck

CD 2 - Track 16

4. When the Saints Get Down

Swing

CD 2 - Track 17

15
16
17
du
du
dut
dut
du
du
dut du du du
du
dut
du
du
du
Bb7
Bdim
F/C
Dmin7
G13
Bb7
Bdim
F/C
Dmin7
15
16
17
18
19
20 all endings
21 last time
du du du
Du dut du dut
du du du
dut
dut
C9
F
Bb/C
F all endings
F last time
G7
C9
F
Bb/C
F all endings
F last time
18
19
20
21
all endings
last time

5. Swingin' at the Riverside

6. New Bossa
CD 2 - Track 19

7. Take the Alternate "A" Train

CD 2 - Track 20

8. Syncopated Samba
CD 2 - Track 21

Scott*MusicPublications*

www.scottmusic.com

Choral Catalog

AIN'T NOBODY

Written & Arranged by Scott Fredrickson

A good swing tune for most choirs using stop-time sections and mostly close four-part harmony.

___3110 SATB (with optional rhythm section parts)

BELIEVE IN YOURSELF

Written & Arranged by Scott Fredrickson

Up-tempo jazz style beginning unison and building to a syncopated SAB finish. A great uplifting text.

___3112 SAB (with optional rhythm section parts)

BRIGHTER DAY

Written & Arranged by Scott Fredrickson

A bright up-tempo jazz style piece extolling the benefits of living each day with hope.

___3119 SATB (with optional rhythm section parts)

CHRISTMAS CAROL COLLECTION

Here We Come A Caroling

Lo How A Rose E're Blooming

O Come O Come Emmanuel

Arranged by Phil Mattson

Three traditional Christmas carols arranged in SATB a cappella, and sparked by Phil's own intriguing style.

___3136 SATB

DA LOVELY

Written & Arranged by Scott Fredrickson

A very mellow Bossa Nova using unison to four-part harmony. A very good change of pace for all choirs.

___3107 SATB (with optional rhythm section parts)

___3123 SSA/Three-Part (with optional rhythm section parts)

GOODBY LOVE

By Ken Kraintz

A revised version of one of Ken's most widely performed choral compositions. A true pop choral standard.

___3141 SATB

Scott*MusicPublications*
www.scottmusic.com

GREAT FEELIN'
Written & Arranged by Scott Fredrickson
One of the best and easiest to sing of the jazz style pieces. Has been performed at many contests and by All-State Choirs.
___3102 SATB (with optional rhythm section parts)
___3120 SSA (with optional rhythm section parts)
___3125 Unison/Two-part (with optional rhythm section parts)

HANUKKAH
Arranged by Gary Fry
Jewish traditions and harmonies are skillfully blended with current pop sounds to produce a wonderful addition to the standard pop Christmas repertoire.
___3137 SATB

HOW ARE WE TO KNOW?
Written & Arranged by Scott Fredrickson
Fast rock tempo style with four-part close harmony and a repeated chorus which builds to an improvised vocal solo with four-part back-up. A good opener.
___3111 SATB (with optional rhythm section parts)

I CAN FLY
Written & Arranged by Scott Fredrickson
A 6/8 "Jazz Waltz" with a two-beat feel building from unison melody to four-part harmony with an improvised vocal scat solo.
___3109 SATB (with optional rhythm section parts)

I HAD A DREAM
Written by Pat Boone & Arranged by Kirby Shaw
Written by as a tribute to Dr. Martin Luther King, and is based on his famous "I had a dream" speech. Arranged in Kirby's own swinging gospel style.
___3135 SATB

I'M FEELIN' RIGHT
By Ken Kraintz
A revised version of one of Ken's all-time jazz-style hits. A real crowd pleaser, and fun to sing.
___3144 SATB

Scott*MusicPublications*
www.scottmusic.com

IT DON'T MEAN A THING
Written & Arranged by Scott Fredrickson
> A sassy jazz style tune that really swings. Each of the three parts is a melody itself, and when put together, almost sounds four-part.
> ___3116 SAB (with optional rhythm section parts)
> ___3121 SSA/Three-Part (with optional rhythm section parts)
> ___3128 Unison/Two-part (with optional rhythm section parts)

IT'S CHRISTMAS
Arranged by Carl Strommen
> Carl has done it again with an exciting arrangement of a delightful Christmas piece which tells about Christmas.
> ___3138 SATB

LEARNING TO LOVE
Written & Arranged by Scott Fredrickson
> Slow unison rock introduction building to a double-time four-part open-voiced chorus. Could be used with two soloists.
> ___3113 SATB (with optional rhythm section parts)

LOOKIN' FOR THE RIGHT WORDS
Written by Frank DeMiero & Arranged by Ken Kraintz
> An up-tempo jazz piece written by Frank DeMiero and arranged in an easy swinging style performed by almost any group.
> ___3146 SATB

LOVING YOU
By Jack Kunz
> A revised version of one of Jack's most widely performed choral compositions. Another pop choral standard.
> ___3142 SATB

MAKIN' All MY DREAMS COME TRUE
By Ken Kraintz
> A medium tempo jazz piece arranged in Ken's own swinging style. A super contest piece.
> ___3143 SATB

Scott*MusicPublications*
www.scottmusic.com

NEW ORLEANS
Arranger by Dave Barduhn

A tasty new version of an old standard arranged in Dave's own unique style.

___3140 SATB

RING THE BELLS AT CHRISTMAS
Written & Arranged by Scott Fredrickson

A lively jazz style Christmas selection for any choir using open-voices harmony building to an improvised solo.

___3108 SATB (with optional rhythm section parts)
___3124 SSA/Three-Part (with optional rhythm section parts)
___3129 Unison/Two-Part (with optional rhythm section parts)

SWINGING AROUND THE XMAS TREE
Written & Arranged by Scott Fredrickson

A catchy up-tempo Christmas tune that is guaranteed to be a lot of fun.

___3115 SATB (with optional rhythm section parts)
___3122 SSA/Three-Part (with optional rhythm section parts)
___3127 Unison/Two-Part (with optional rhythm section parts)

THAT'S THE WAY YA DO IT
Written & Arranged by Scott Fredrickson

Jazz shuffle with some changing meter using close four-part harmony. A fun novelty for any group.

___3106 SATB (with optional rhythm section parts)
___3126 Unison/Two-Part (with optional rhythm section parts)

UNDER THE RAINBOW
Arranged by Clark Gassman

A lilting 3/4 melody arranged into a delightful choral version by one of America's top arrangers.

___3139 SATB

WE NEED MORE LOVE IN THE WORLD
Written & Arranged by Scott Fredrickson

A four-part chorus is repeated in this rock-style piece leading to a unison contrapuntal melody and improvised solo.

___3117 SATB (with optional rhythm section parts)

Scott*MusicPublications*
www.scottmusic.com

WHEN I'M NEAR YOU
Written & Arranged by Scott Fredrickson
> A good change of pace for any group, using Bossa Nova time with some changing meter.
> ___3103 SATB (with optional rhythm section parts)

WHERE DO WE GO?
Written & Arranged by Scott Fredrickson
> Changing meter Latin style building from unison melodic lines to four-part close harmony. A challenging composition for an experienced group.
> ___3101 SATB (with optional rhythm section parts)

WILL YOU LOVE ME?
Written & Arranged by Scott Fredrickson
> A very pretty ballad for female solo and four-part chorus. Could work well for a large group also.
> ___3114 SATB (with optional rhythm section parts)

WINDS OF LOVE
Written & Arranged by Scott Fredrickson
> A slow a cappella ballad introduction building to a double-time Latin tempo with unison melody in all parts.
> ___3105 SATB (with optional rhythm section parts)

YOU ARE
Written & Arranged by Scott Fredrickson
> One of the few really swing ballads. Chorus sings tight inner-voiced four-part lines, with occasional solo parts.
> ___3118 SATB (with optional rhythm section parts)

YOU'LL BE THERE
By Jack Kunz
> A moving ballad that flows melodically and harmonically through many textures to produce an exciting arrangement that is destined to be one of Jack's most widely performed compositions.
> ___3145 SATB

Scott*MusicPublications*
www.scottmusic.com

YOUR LOVE
Written & Arranged by Scott Fredrickson

A fine ballad for an experienced group using two to five-part close-voiced chromatic harmony.

___3104 SATB (with optional rhythm section parts)

Books

SCAT SINGING METHOD
By Dr. Scott Fredrickson

The Method contains full written instructions and two cassette tapes containing a step-by-step guide to successfully teach vocal improvisation. These techniques have been proven effective by thousands of college and high school instructors. Each Method also contains eight performable compositions and arrangements to practice the skills learned. Separate vocal and rhythm section parts are also available.

___3801 Scat Method With Two CDs
___3802 Scat Method Vocal Parts
___3803 Scat Method Rhythm Pack
___3804 Scat Method Rhythm Tracks

POPULAR CHORAL HANDBOOK
By Dr. Scott Fredrickson

This Handbook contains over 350 pages of techniques and concepts for Pop, Jazz and Show Choir style and interpretation that have been proven effective through years of use in graduate schools and choral conducting seminars and workshops. Each Handbook comes with a CD containing numerous musical examples notated in the book. Topics include: developing the appropriate choral tone, rehearsal techniques, conducting, chord tuning, rhythmic intensity, melodic interpretation, repertoire selection, programming decisions, and much more.

___3805 Popular Choral Handbook With Two CDs

Popular Choral Handbook

New Techniques
for
Pop, Jazz, and Show Choir Directors

by

Dr. Scott Fredrickson

Here is what Top Choral Educators are saying about the *Popular Choral Handbook*:

Everything a contemporary choral director would need - from the very general to the detailed.
   • Deb Stolar - Pelham, NH

One of the only texts that contains all of the necessary elements to produce quality choruses.
   • Ginny Bomil - Dracut, MA

A well-rounded resource for all aspects of choral singing. Concepts can be applied to all choral ensembles. The rehearsal techniques section is GOLD for the new or experienced director.
   • Lyn DeCosta - East Falmouth High School, MA

If you are going to buy one book dealing with popular and jazz vocal music, make it this one. It covers everything you'll ever need to know about dealing with the jazz or pop vocal ensemble.
   • Bob Chadwick - Auburn Middle School, MA

This is an unbelievable resource book. All of the problems I had last year with my choirs could have been addressed just by an initial perusal of this text. I will have this book on my desk.
   • Dan Wulf - Watertown High School, MA

This text broke down concepts in such a common sense way sometimes it made me stop and say, "Why didn't I think of that?"
   • Carolyn Alzapiedi - Hudson, MA

Popular Choral Handbook

by

Dr. Scott Fredrickson

Table of Contents

Popular Choral Handbook

8.   Intonation and Tuning
          Listening in Tune
          Singing in Tune
              Atmospheric
              Acoustic
              Emotional
              Physical
              Technical
              Rehearsal
9.   Rehearsal Techniques
          Attitude
          Technique
          Environment
          Peak Experience
          Levels of Success
          Closure
          Mental Alertness and Attention Span
          Introducing a New Piece of Music
          Goals
          Feedback
          Directions
          Correcting Mistakes and Problems
          Power and Leadership
              Punitive power
              Compensatory power
              Conditioned power
              Traditional leadership
              Functional leadership
              Personal leadership
              Formal power system
              Informal power system
              Fear
              Respect
              Positive peer pressure
              Positive reinforcement
          Seating Arrangement
              Sectional seating
              Small groups
              Scrambled seating
              Circular seating

Popular Choral Handbook

Warm-ups
    Pace
    Vocal Instruction Throughout the Rehearsal
    Sight-reading
    Use of Sectionals
        Individual voice part
        Small groups
    Use of the Rhythm Section

10. Conducting the Ensemble
    Use of Traditional and New Terminology
    Use of Descriptive Imagery
    Physical Conducting Technique
        Posture
        Internal beat
        Precision
        Initial attack
        Beat patterns
        Ambidexterity
        Conducting planes
        Intensity plane
        Visualization through body language
        Visualization through facial expression
        Physical imagery
        Memory layers
    Score Study
        Prior study
        Form
        Melodic considerations
        Harmonic considerations
        Rhythmic considerations
        Texture
        Textual considerations
    Individual voice part considerations
        Tone quality considerations
        Dynamic considerations

11. Stylistic Considerations Affecting Interpretation
    Pop Style
    Swing Style
    Latin Style
    Rock Style
    Broadway Show Style
    Country Style
    Ballad Style

Popular Choral Handbook

12. Rhythmic Intensity
> Rhythmic Consistency and Placement
>> Inattention on the part of the director
>> Inexperienced rhythm section players
>> Inexperienced accompanist
>> Overly experienced accompanist
>> Beat consistency
>> Subdivision of the beat
>> Rushing
>> Dragging
>> On the beat
>> Ahead of the beat
>> Behind the beat
> Teaching Rhythm First
> Interpretation of Traditional Rhythms
> Tempo in Relation to Style and Musicality
> Rhythmic Phrasing
> Accents
>> Written accents
>> Breath accent
>> H accent
>> Heimlich accent
>> D or L accent
>> Tenuto with space accent
>> Rushing
>> Note separation
> Attacks
>> Tempo
>> Style
>> Consonants
>> Vowels
>> Lyrics
>> Precision
> Releases
> Syncopation
> Miscellaneous Rhythmic Considerations

Popular Choral Handbook

13. Linear Intensity Through Melodic Interpretation
>   Intensity Changes Within the Melodic Line
>   Tone Color Contrast Within the Melodic Line
>   Intensity Changes on Longer Duration Notes
>   Intensity Changes on Repeated Notes
>   Counter-melodies
>   Inner-moving Notes
>>   Accent
>>   Dynamics
>
>   Tone color change
>>   Polyphony vs. Homophony
>>   Lyrics
>>>   Key words
>>>   Connector words
>>>   Filler words
>>
>>   Phrasing
>>   Jazz Nuances, Inflections, and Ornaments
>>>   Fall-off
>>>   Ascending smear
>>>   Ascending glissando
>>>   Plop
>>>   Doit
>>>   Ghost note
>>>   Shake
>>>   Flip

14. Chordal Intensity Through Harmonic Considerations
>   Vertical Chord Structure vs. Horizontal Line
>   Levels of Dissonance vs. Consonance
>   Chord Tuning
>>   Energy level
>>   Tempo
>>   Texture
>>   Chord span and texture
>>   Style
>>   Volume
>>   Pitch placement and tendency
>>   Tone color
>>   Rhythmic placement
>
>   Blend and Balance Through Vocal Color
>>   Individual voice part dynamics

Popular Choral Handbook

Pronunciation and vowel placement
    Rhythmic accuracy
    Tone color
    Levels of dissonance vs. consonance
    Changing blend
    Use of vibrato
    Approach dissonant chords
    Quartal chords
    Clusters and closed-voiced chords
    Textual considerations
15. Overall Intensity Through Contrast
    Building Contrast Through Dynamics
        Span
        Range
        Flow
        Group size and experience
        Style
        Tempo
        Lyrical Content
        Melodic content
        Dissonance vs. consonance
        Experiments with dynamics
    Building Contrast Through Tone Color
        Span
        Range
        Flow
    Building Contrast Within Repetition
        Dynamic ranges between phrases
        Intensity change within phrases
    Building Contrast Within Structure
16. Repertoire Selection
    The Art of Repertoire Selection
    Number of Voice Parts, Range, and Tessitura
    Degree of Difficulty
    Quality and Musical Taste
17. Programming Decisions
    Types of Organization
        Chronological
        Thematic
    Pacing
    Building to a Climax

Popular Choral Handbook

Dr. Scott Fredrickson has over 30 years experience in higher education and experience in the music industry and holds degrees in Music Education from Cal-State University Fullerton, Business Administration from Pepperdine University, Jazz, and Music Business Administration from the University of Northern Colorado. His compositions and arrangements have been heard on local and national radio and television, and are being performed regularly in the United States and many other countries. Fredrickson has worked as a composer, arranger, director, and performer at theme parks, dinner theaters and corporate shows, and numerous commercial projects. He has produced and engineered numerous albums of pop and jazz vocal music and is in much demand as a clinician, guest conductor, and festival adjudicator throughout the United States, Canada, and Europe. His Scat Singing Method has been received enthusiastically by choral directors, and his articles on pop, jazz and show choir techniques have appeared in national educational journals and magazines. He is President of Scott Music Publications, and former editor and publisher of Pop, Jazz & Show Choir Magazine and has just completed a new choral music education text book entitled Popular Choral Handbook. He is the former President and Executive Director of the Music & Entertainment Industry Educators Association and is a member of ASCAP. He has also consulted with and chaired numerous university music business programs and now lives and works in New Orleans, Louisiana.

Printed in the United States
48228LVS00005B/89-112

9 780962 017704